Stunt Double

poems by

Elizabeth Garcia

Finishing Line Press
Georgetown, Kentucky

Stunt Double

ACKNOWLEDGMENTS

"Atlanta to Salt Lake," *Fire in the Pasture: 21st Century Mormon Poets*.
Reprinted in *Dialogue: A Journal of Mormon Thought*.
"Dad Feels Like Daniel Boone Inside," "Rereading Bulfinch, I think I
understand Echo," Penumbra Poetry Contest winner, *Seven Hills Review*
"Leaving California," *491 Magazine*
"An Hour of PBS," *Boxcar Poetry Review*
"Dead Dog Poem," *Red River Review*
"An alarm sounds at Barnes & Noble," formerly "Inertia," *Poets and Artists*
"Adjusting," *Irreantum*; Reprinted in *Fire in the Pasture: 21st Century
Mormon Poets*
"Labor Day, One Year Married," *Stone, River, Sky: An Anthology of Georgia
Poems*
"God as Intern," *Irreantum*. Nominated for Pushcart Prize. Reprinted in *Fire
in the Pasture: 21st Century Mormon Poets*.
"What I will now do for you," *Yellow Chair Review*
"Nineteen, with a Fireman," *Autumn Sky Review*

Editor: Christen Kincaid

Cover Art: Elizabeth Garcia

Author Photo: Rommel Garcia

Cover Design: Elizabeth Maines

Printed in the USA on acid-free paper.
Order online: www.finishinglinepress.com
also available on amazon.com

Author inquiries and mail orders:
Finishing Line Press
P. O. Box 1626
Georgetown, Kentucky 40324
U. S. A.

Table of Contents

While I am living in the other's joy, I do not feel primordial joy. It does not issue live from my "I." Neither does it have the character of once having lived like remembered joy. But still much less is it merely fantasized without actual life. This other subject is primordial although I do not experience it as primordial. In my non-primordial experience I feel, as it were, led by a primordial one not experienced by me but still there, manifesting itself in my non-primordial experience.

Thus empathy is a kind of act of perceiving. [. . .] This is how human beings comprehend the psychic life of their fellows. Also as believers they comprehend the love, the anger, and the precepts of their God in this way; and God can comprehend people's lives in no other way.

—Edith Stein, "On the Problem of Empathy"

Atlanta to Salt Lake
—for Sally

Prose will not capture some people, the way
they drift. You can only see them dragging
their furniture through Wyoming night,
down a dark throat of road, the ice
clear and slick. We stopped to sleep in a solitary
town: Rawlins, Wyoming. Ahead:

a slow hundred miles of snow. (Things ahead
are always murky, but we go anyway,
forward.) Oklahoma was first, the solitary
landscape scarred with arthritic trees, as if dragged
up by their bones. We stopped only twice,
once at a motel with "crap" on the walls, and all night

she couldn't sleep, fearing what other nights
("hookers and pimps") had left in the sheets. And still ahead
of us, Nebraska flats and the Wyoming ice
a vast white cliché. It wasn't the way
I expected, but an easier slope for dragging
that U-haul than I-15. Just solitary.

Only a semi every few miles. We played laptop solitaire
by turns—her black skirt in the window shading her like night,
blocking the sun, while my toes went numb—dragging
the load away from failed relationships, hoping ahead
for clarity, like Thelma and Louise. But that's not the way
it works. Still, we ate at that truck stop the night before. Ice

shrapneled our faces. Her dad phoned to warn us of icy
roads that could lead to cliffs and a solitary
death where our car might "blow up. That would suck." His way
of cheering her up—and it worked. That night
we laughed through the rattlesnake backscratchers, Dead Head
T-shirts, Jesus figures, stuffed pigs dressed in camo, dragging

ourselves to warm beds in a decent motel. Then that dragging
day through whitewash, WY, horizons of ice,
to Rock Springs, shouts, and a Pizza Hut buffet. Ahead
was Utah, final destination for her solitary
path without men, though every night
she would think of the same one. But that's the way

it works—in circles. The way she came dragging
back home, still obscured by night, months later, the ice
still thick inside. More solitary. Less looking ahead.

Rereading Bulfinch, I think I understand Echo

Eventually we all evaporate
into stories. And what is mine:
Loving a man who loved himself, a private

woody wasting away. Not a rape
(no wing-whipped thighs, no bovine-grunting whine).
Eventually, we all evaporate

into voices, cries that punctuate,
intertwine our thick denial, like vines,
we loved men who loved themselves, a private

thing shared, mourning what's too late
to try: drug him to docility with wine.
Eventually we all evaporate;

why not sprinkle amnesia, defecate
on his dinner, stare him into stone?
I loved a man who loved himself. Private

martyrdom is white-armed, bare-throat ache
I could have eased by infamy, a spine.
Eventually we all evaporate
(from loving men who love themselves) in private.

Leaving California
—for my mother

She bundled up her baby, all her mother things, her books,
till the blue wagon was full. Her husband drove the whole way,

so she watched the desert, how it stood still for minutes
at a time, only moved when she wasn't looking, like her life,

plucked,   because he had a dream:
they would live in Georgia, where she knew no one,

always thought of race riots and burnings. She only knew
the bite of snow, its burial, freezing eyelash to shard.

And hills over ocean, how fog soothes the spike of city,
blurs the tops of bridges, so you learn to imagine half of everything,

and how it ends. This would keep her looking forward,
watching the green deepen slowly through Texas, cling to her throat

in Louisiana, where she rolled the windows down and clenched her
    jaw
against the stammer of potholes. Kept her leaning forward

to each town, each traffic light. She didn't know how far apart
they could be, how much could be forgotten between each one,

like the lightning they had raced through Kansas, the metal
    calligraphy
of roof along the road, the snap of trees, like his pocketful of
    toothpicks.

Virginity Checks
Cairo—March 9, 2011

Is it rape to tent
the screen of flesh with a woody finger,
and not go through? She'll clench

her eyes—*could be*
worse—her father felled across her mother
like a palm tree,

bark marking all
her body. This, she imagined, hearing
sawing through the wall,

vowing she would never
let herself turn to dust. Watching
her mother blown with every

open door, collected
in the corners. *It's over in a second,*
she thinks, petrified.

Dad Feels Like Daniel Boone Inside

I discover this in the ER, his shirt opened up
to EKG sensors, to skin I haven't seen in years,

all the hair a white I remember: grandpa,
naked at the bathroom door, *Doris! Turn off that dishwasher!*

not knowing I was sitting there with my pudding pop
watching the soaps.

We've been here for an hour now, my mother
answering the nurse for him, and hovering,

so he gives up. Makes the radiology tech tilt his bed to the TV
so he can find something cowboy-looking, the colors muted—

a prairie woman with a bouffant 'do and blue eye shadow.
The colored lines of the monitors all undulate—

all but one, flat and blue. I joke to Mom: *Is that for brain activity?*
She grins, and he's oblivious, intent on how the drunk

will finish chopping all that wood: Boone's justice,
meted out for some sin I've missed in the plot,

the volume pointed only at him—though I could make up
some offense in black and white put right, the squabble

of some village where gunslingers flick out clichés
with nimble wrists, tipping hats to ladies who sashay through town

and bonnet back their words, who clang with suppertime,
scratching out their lives with washboard knuckles. The place

where Boone's voice resonates through the woods,
deep and mellow, the mountain lion and the lamb

warm their hands to its amber glow,
and my father's heart returns to sinus rhythm.

Wonder Woman's First Stunt Double

was a man. With a hairy chest
like lichen, the great tundra of his torso
packed into spandex: Let's shrink-wrap Siberia
and put it in a tube of toothpaste.
So he spends an hour in his trailer, wincing,
thinking of his mother,

one foot on the tub, sliding nylons up her leg
front to back, front to back.
How she gathered them in a bunch, her toes pointed,
feet arcing up and through like dolphins,
then tunneling through their dark water,
safe and hidden from the upper world.

How she hummed as they swam.
He could never pick out the tune,
some absent-minded scattering of notes
only she knew. And when he somersaults off that roof,
he feels how far away she is, the wide gulf of air
beneath him, the great oak of his body
reaching out to tuck, to cradle.

An Hour of PBS
—for Rommel

We're watching Darwin struggle between awe of rotten bird,
the fecund seeds hidden in the gut—and doubt,
the barnacle lodged in his back.

His wife pushes him through darkness
toward immortality, secret of life, corona
to light up all her children in one room.

But it cannot eclipse those half graves.
Each time, he buckles, and I wonder
what heat and pressure the plates

of the face require, why my father
never wept when he buried children,
one by the wall of our house in San Fernando, in a shoebox.

He blared the TV upstairs, let the rest of us
place paper flowers on the grave. Let my mother
heave alone, her body emptied.

I'd like to hear what sounds he tried to drown.
Wonder if I climbed those stairs, if I'd find Darwin
weeping there. Something worth the dark.

Finding Abel

I

It wasn't like him
to nap.

There he was,
sprawled.

Red petals flecked
his cheek,

his ear   *so this*
          is what it looks like:

          Eve, sleeping
          with her eyes open.

What I don't tell her:
something glittered

in the grass—
his hair

rooted in bony
clump,

bone like any
sheep.

He left the way he came:
head first, fisted.

II

This is woman's work.
The proper work of fingers:

Gently wash the arm. The hand.
The dirt beneath the nails.

The cake of it on calloused heels.
The hidden flesh, soft and white.

A need for symmetry
that comes after your own body

has buckled, fallen to the ground
like a coat of skins.

After it has lain there, crumpled
while you lie with your guilt,

let it enter you: *this
is the world   I   brought us to*

that delicious bite
grown bitter in the mouth.

We smooth the stubbled skin.
Comb burrs from the hair,

woolly as the sheep
he'd stroke

at the nape, staring
at the meadow, how the wind

trailed its fingers
through the tall grass.

I knew this one was mine,
this way:

he wanted to watch
all day, the world

lambent, still.
Now,

just still.
The purple stain

a hand,
claiming him.

Dead Dog Poem

I would click on the hazard lights.

I would ease to a stop. And if the driver
close behind was on his phone, or watching

the train that raced us on the left,

I would let him crash into me—
so there would be two to stop for you,

to watch you heaving, to argue

what to do at night when there's no owner,
no neighborhood around—just woods,

and one bright gas station.

Maybe he would have a gun.
Maybe I would have a little more to say.

An alarm sounds at Barnes & Noble

*The earthquake that struck Japan on Friday was so
powerful that it actually moved the whole planet by 25cm.*
—*The Daily Mail*

From rows and rows of books,
voices clatter like telegraphs,
the ceiling screeches jazz, a tinny horn—an alarm
peels out of the trumpet like an osprey,
circling its wounded mate, the circular song
it scries, vibrato-long, you'd think it would shatter
the glass of the lake below, a giant
burst of moths into the sky.

And then it stops. No one's paused
to warn, "Get out, a fire!" Or stumbled by,
checking chairs to empty patrons. Or stammered
a "Hey, Hey! Stop him!" Or choked
on pronoun—it was a her
with hair like wire.
We all go back to our books.
I think, *how easy is inertia.*

Willing the kid outside to keep on digging
his nose, the cars to get green lights,
the pansies to shudder just so,
flashing gold, the man with loaded shopping cart
to flow like river, skirting smooth
around rocks, willing the world to keep
centripetal force, her center pedal on the gas
just so, her center flower blooming,
slowly, slowly unfolding, yes,
her axis tilted just so,
you know she wants to stay this way forever.

What I will now do for you
—to my friend who has lost her child

Nurses slam into gurneys.
Pills sprinkle the air. Red Jello Rorschachs
stain the walls, outside, a lady and her dog are tangled
in the trees, the leash gone limp, the chubby cop and the thug
with droopy drawers cling to the wire fence like wilted
laundry, and in kitchens everywhere, cooks have lopped off
fingers, the sous chefs swim in a sea of metal, pots and pans
chiming their confusion and in some hotel, a pair of lovers
thinks they've reached some out of body free-fall, and they
splash, tractor trailers grind and twist on the highway in some
slow angle, cars thrust forward, drivers pump their brakes,
splay their hands, their noses against the glass to see
the whole world floating,
some apocalypse.

Tell me how long to leave them hanging there.
(I know this much: they must relearn their bodies.
How to maneuver. What is up or down.)
And when you're ready,
just before the atmosphere has burned away,
just before that last desperate gasp for air,
we'll let the earth start back its turning,
let them all drop in a dusty heap,
thud to their knees in strange backyards,
plunk deep into ocean, sinking with brick feet,
skid down some dotted desert road,
spine on bony spine.

We'll give instructions:
Stand, bruised.
Brush off the dirt and walk the long way back
to what you were doing.
You'll have time to think of it again.
Carry your broken thermometers,
your bent whisks.
Don't ask why, just walk.
If it's hot, strip off your sweater.
Wipe the sweat from your forehead.
Bear the sear of blisters starting at your heels
because your shoes aren't right for this.

Nineteen, with a Fireman

This is the age you shed your ideals like a seed coat
the moment you are desired. It will start

in the backseat, with root (your white looping his brown)
a tendril up the waist, and soon the body: xylem

you have reached daylight heat (he's a Fire Man!)
and forgotten:

You are not alone.
The others (three) will stare straight ahead,

focus on Skynard twanging from the dash,
the blur of trees, the river they've planned on tubing down

still miles ahead. Tammy
will chatter away to his terse friends

of college courses, things to do in Tallahassee
while you (and He!) are flushed, smoldering

next to her, her frail body
snagged on adolescence like a burr,

swallowed by a too large T-shirt,
years of bathroom afternoons, dredging up

that giant salad, those hospital nights,
her mother's squeak, her father's boom,

till the eyes burn with the strain,
that lovely, familiar burn

of finding emptiness,
the gourd hollow,

of reminding herself
I know how to be alone.

Watching The Elephant Man, Age 13

What you end up remembering isn't always the same
as what you have witnessed.
—Julian Barnes

I
The burlap sags,
 like wax,
  melted

jagged holes
 where eyes
  should be,

the cloak,
 a hulking
  indeterminacy

the cane,
 the dragging,
  anvil-slow

the hat,
 like any respectable
  fellow.

II
Unsheathed, he has a head
 and a shoulder, and a mass
  anything made of matter

or something that has mass
 and takes up space and somewhere
  between anything and something

is a neck, and the frame
　　　is a circular, semantic argument,
　　　　　muscle and bone fused together,

the early man made of clay
　　　unfinished, when the creator remembered
　　　　　there was something in the oven, burning.

III
He is wearing a suit,　　speaking
　　　into the mirror *the lord is my shepherd, I shall not want*
　　　　　every consonant labored, thick-tongued,

when they crash (his friends) into his small room
　　　drunken, pin him down,
　　　　　lift the shrieking woman like a battering ram

towards his face for a kiss, his eyes bulging, petrified
　　　with the woman's horror of him.
　　　　　And after the party,

they leave him there, shirtless, wheezing,
　　　every breath like Sisyphus, until the last,
　　　　　when he lies down to sleep. Prostrate,

like anyone else. And as the weight of that mass
　　　bears down on his throat, his spine,
　　　　　bears him down to sleep forever,

he's thinking of the soft hand
of the woman who smiled that one time,
that soft back of the hand

with no purpose but for touching, smooth as stone,
as petals. What another life could give him: forever
to touch and be touched.

To My Husband, 11pm

> *"... that in your very*
> *arms I still*
> *can think of you."*
> —Robert Creeley, *"The Act of Love"*

You are shuttling into that world again,
and I am waiting here, watching you sleep.
What spiral are you shadowing into, what widening

tunnel away from me? Is it the cavern
of that first girl you wanted to light up?
You are shuttling into that world again . . .

all your time a rod you've leaned against a tree, its line
spooled and ready while you burrow in for ore, dive deep
into that shadowy spiral, your widened

journey to earth's core to search for your beginning,
oil lamp raised, naming formations: Side of Bacon. Lion's Pelt.
You are shuttling into that world again,

loosening its soil, and I will be a woman with a cane
when you return, all the words I've steeped
spiraling into the shadows away from me, widening

like galaxies, the empty space between.
If we were as young as our tongues, as supple,
I could shuttle into your thoughts again,
and we could spiral into the shadows, widened.

Dad hangs onto old things like a lover

The typewriter. Red velvet lining
of its case matted down. Each key
mushroom-colored, stiffening with rust.

Sewing machine, circa 1920,
its iron pump's pull and thrust
the *fort - da* of loving.

It's reverse psychology:
keep them around collecting dust
so she thinks you couldn't care less.

Keep the broken computer like a bust
of Antony. And every look into its loveless eyes,
you see your fear of losing,

of the Body finally admitting
You don't deserve me
as she turns away in disgust.

Adjusting

Somewhere in the pile of plastic wrap, stacks
of yellow bowls, blue-lidded pyrex, the metal-slick clink

of gifts we hope will last for years and several children,
is the woman you married, the girl you loved

before she became Woman of the House, Your
House, the garage too crowded

for two cars. Her arm stretches across your bed like Iowa
before she touches flesh. And you reach out

with closed eyes, hold her bone warmth, not knowing
she is still outside, trying to think of words

to name it all. Remembering: it was Adam
who got the naming power, made Eve

Mother before she could be Girl. How long
would it take for her to turn

toward that sound? Did she sense the girl
inside, the muted memory, the leaves

in her periphery, twitching? Or just
hunger, a stomach growling

for self, a woman with all things given to her
who wanted. And when she ate the fruit,

she devoured the Memory in its flesh—
her elusive Daughter-ness—

sucked her History from its pit,
licked clean her sticky palms,

her living fingertips, stretched them out behind her
to touch God's hand.

Ode to that truck driver in 1978

You probably had things
on your mind. Like Waylon Jennings.
Making it to Dothan
before dark. Your wife you hadn't
made love to, at least
two months. And fields rolling past
your window, yellow land
you wanted to roll in with her. And
a house, sagging in
the trees, a dirty white. Then:
red flutter, highway's
edge. Right foot off the gas,
(a reflex after rodents,
deer) and passing, second glance:

blonde pigtails, red
jumper, baby squat. You eyed
mirrors, hit the brakes,
then, hard, skidded rocks
to stop. And nothing either
way for miles of twilight glimmer.
Flicked your hazards. Climbing
down, you scanned the yard, gleaming
windows, walking stiff,
from aching muscles, nice and slow, if
someone noticed you.
And she was watching you. With blue
brilliant eyes. And tucked
in pudgy hands, a yellow cup.

Right in the road.
You held out your calloused hand.
She took it, too. Just
going for a walk across
the yard, familiar rocks.
To chicken, biscuit smell. You knocked
the wobbly screen, gut
rumbling. Then: a silhouette
of woman wrapped in apron,
fisting a rag. Halved by newsprint,
a man sat behind her,
little boy on the floor
scattering trucks, a couch
sprawling out you wanted to slouch

your bones into. Instead: "Is this your little
girl?" Back inside your rig moments
later, it was okay they didn't ask
you in to eat. You saw the woman's face,
how lost she was, remembering how futile
all her stirring, how quiet it had been,
the calling out of names: *Wash up, now!*
You left her in an O of thought, sifting
all she hadn't done, like sand, like flour.
Now, your engine smooths the gaps between
the unexpected. And when you're home, you'll flip
your hat aside, grab your glowing wife
around her waist, kiss her till she loosens,
recalls how close she was to dropping life
to ditch, to dust up like a yellow cup.

Labor Day, One Year Married

The day we carted river rock from front yard
to back, I was thinking of Courbet's *Stonebreakers,*
its muted blues and grays washed out

against the bright, and you knew the sun
was beating on their backs—on ours,
each shovelful hunched over, clouds of dust

escaping rock bodies like souls.
I shoveled into a mesh wastebasket,
hoping it would sift the dirt, then buckled

over its fullness to rattle out the pebbles
into wheelbarrow. My husband
shoveled directly there, and when its apron filled,

carted to the back, wobbling drunk under the weight.
I don't know how many shovelfuls I'd strained against, committed,
before noticing the quiet that had settled on my shoulders

for some time. That stopping, I knew he was back there, sitting.
Breathing. Hiding how the weight he'd added on
was bearing down on him, lungs filling with the rocks,

shovel by shovel, wishing he'd spent that extra hundred bucks
for someone else to do this, thinking that one year ago,
we were young, and no one minded all that rock.

God as Intern

I

Twilight: a great scab
crusted over the land,

a red line
seething, an end

of oozing, deceptive
stillness. We itch

to make it palpable,
this waiting, caught

between end and beginning.
Did the first of these

bring nostalgia, a yearning
more for past worlds

or the next? We think always
of endings in this half

light, of loss, forgetting
that evening came first,

darkness before
the light, the morning

wrapping up the great
project, God's gray head

napping on a crooked elbow,
dreaming of formulas.

II

Before declaring
it was good, eons before

there was a before,
how many scraps did it take

to learn measure twice,
cut once?

And what paternal tips given:
Water down the marble

to cool the spinning blade.
(We don't want explosions.)

How many crooked bookshelves
of redwood, grooves that fit

in only one combination,
one leaning post that needed

propping, how many drafts
of diagram to dissect, recalculate,

the paper rubbed transparent
from erasures, and how much forgiveness

before mastering perpetual motion of rivers,
the great slow pendulum of moon rock?

Elizabeth Cranford Garcia is a stay-at-home-mom of two young children, formerly an Assistant Professor of English Literature and Composition at Georgia Perimeter College in Atlanta, Georgia. She received her BA in Humanities from Brigham Young University in 2000 and her MA in English Literature from Valdosta State University in 2003 before teaching for seven years, and began writing and studying poetry in earnest in 2007. She won her first contest in 2008, and has since been published in *Irreantum, Boxcar Poetry Review, Poets and Artists, Segullah Literary Journal, 491 Magazine, Penwood Review,* and *The Resurrectionist,* among others. She was nominated for a Pushcart Prize in 2010, and won both first and second place awards in the Penumbra Poetry Contest for *Seven Hills Review* in 2014. Her work has also been included in a recent anthology, *Fire in the Pasture: 21st Century Mormon Poets,* 2011, and in *Stone, River, Sky: an Anthology of Georgia Poems* by Negative Capability Press. She has been a past editor of *The Reach of Song,* the anthology for the Georgia Poetry Society, and currently serves as Poetry Editor for *Segullah Literary Journal.* She spends most of her time being mommy to two toddlers and keeping up with *Walking Dead* episodes with her husband in Acworth, Georgia.

www.ingramcontent.com/pod-product-compliance
Lightning Source LLC
LaVergne TN
LVHW091234080426
835509LV00009B/1275